PROTECTION

Robert Bal

ISBN: 978-1-915079-46-6

Cover designed by Aaron Kent

Edited and typeset by Aaron Kent

Broken Sleep Books Ltd
Rhydwen,
Talgarreg,
SA44 4HB
Wales

Contents

Protection

Robert Bal

for charanpal

nineteen eighty two

at every get together, when
everybody went away together,
every christmas and new years
as if we didn't know the way
it felt but how it felt to feel
as if we'd never say a word
- i always kept the score.

at the front of the system
was a word, a hand pushed
through the curtain drew
and pressed against the pane
to ward you off, in the spirit
of protection - a racket run
upon the self, a metabolic
wrench turned tight inside
to keep the wrong unspoken.

i learned to stop my gob up,
choked on the need to steel
myself against the fear of ending
up sent back to where i'd come
from, alone, pushed out of sight -
i tried so hard to get it right,
but with no way to get it right
or ever give up trying.

the remit of the system learned
will always be deterrent: a rabid
sacrificial move i held inside
as if ordained by imperial benign,
as if constrained to march bestride
the trench of rule brittania made,

the tighten up and move along,
the new one two to leave behind
an old country not meant for me,
gone long before i ever came,
and such a shame to never have
belonged in an english afternoon.

six foot from the autocrat

life on the a4 verge came solitary;
i found myself ancillary to a knighted city,
the lesser london they call the greater,
the how and slow of my despair.

> my people came fresh off the boat
> with ears alert for the epoch's howl,
> the tax we paid in blood
> to live beneath the crown, unloved,
> double backed to bend in vain
> and work the airplane vapour trail
> - to try to stay connected. but then i
> was there, not theirs but there,
> the soil in which the beat dropped,
> a seed not meant for any harvest,
> a shoot to be cut down to size.

the roots of every frown was in the eyes;
all value in the mirror's dream of one day
somehow being clean, kept busy proving it
untrue. this is how they taught me too,
a british education, one in speaking down,
the father tongue of knowing difference,
gliding out one side a smiling mouth,
then out the other, for the other one,
the rhythm of the bloodless rose
and all the way it licks you, in english,
for the english won the right to put it on you -
all that morass of what they assigned you,
all that soggy architecture, all those mossy
strings attached before you ever breathed
for you to be a blight upon their streets.

a braid of retail selves on show in need of space
enough just to pull the other one, to take your turn
to disappear from a world made for them who have it
made, who terrorize the territories for their trade,
who bomb in waves that roll through generations
who reveal themselves revolted, by themselves,
left begging for affiliation with those who drowned
them out; i was propelled up from the floor to dance,
compelled as if by chance to stay and hear
how i'd been played like i was not a person.

dusty plastic orange chair

i shed a world to come from there, but
there's no welcome home for me,
just a droning in the head like smoke
backed up inside a blocked-up chimney,
a gravid cloud from which i dropped
and rolled to smother all conviction.

i was the hopeless case of all the space
they always took to keep me in my place,
a homophone so dear they ran me down,
then strung me up, all dun, familiar,
stretched out on the rack of an ancestral
village name, forgotten, left to cobble sounds
together from the distant pound of firing pins,
betrayed, a can kicked down the road,
airmail sent in time of famine, a train delayed,
impatient on their waiting track of bones.

my hooded eyes were always serving, underhand
and looking out from under, always under supervision,
swerving just to break a little, to find a more efficient
way to say, yeah, i think that i can do it, so let me try
the move you make, that military, ordered, march,
and i was on the spot: a tragic little soldier.

inside my head i said it to myself: that i was more
like them, and so the weight, a second, rendered
light, ascended, all sent up; i got it straight,
picked a drum and beat it down, drove my rank
and file across the floor, the face of war reflecting
back from every sorry angle, with no way to fight
their clever tread of never having turned upon the spit,
of never having been spat on, of never having heard
the voice come out, come out, in a frightened whisper.

when a go is what they give you

i had to get vouched for to get inside.
if i could get vouched for i could go on in,
go overboard, go all in, go across
the windswept ocean. i dropped my eyes:
they watched unblinking as the door swung shut
behind a great divide now bridged. the disparity
absorbed in silence. a face that did not belong.

i never brought it round again. i dropped
the frightened whisper - tried a lisp instead,
a different laugh, a thinner lip, tried to pass,
a destiny apparent in all the ways i kept
on trying to get inside though i had got an in,
as if required to model how i wanted
to be seen, the way they never would.

they loved to see me itch to bounce.
they kept me brooding, kept me tethered
to my colour, mispronounced and out to sea
where they could watch me drowning.

this is the bruise i have uncovered; the years
i spent entombed and lonely in that green
unpleasant land, their every need a fresh
demand, and no one ever told me different.

i worked as if a farmer ploughing his own field,
as if the crop was mine and by it i'd be fed,
but i was an ox, instead, harnessed tightly in the yoke.

one nil to them

we come from everywhere their toxic whip
has licked unclean: the windsor chair, held
up by hungry legions, still landing blows today.

we are the foreign smoke in the london eye.
we work to keep up with a rotten upper lip,
a bubonic paragon we harrowed up the hill
upon our backs, a nonesuch mask we've all seen
slip, but stay discreet enough to look away in silence.

we stay on task, in touch, unseen. we stay off-balance,
one foot up and fighting hard to bring it down,
in place, before the other. the thrill we feel is in the hope
of one day ending any need to hope, or get ahead -
not to get there first, but just a head, to feel the whole
length of the neck one day without the need
to wind it in. this is our rank and grave conscription.

the lizard smiles as we get in line to have a sass instilled
in us, provided on the public health, a general anaesthetic,
a wondrous aesthetic of apparent wealth, the guarantor
of every breath we give for all their cause as it escapes
our bodies. and there it is: one nil to them, without a strike

on goal. the toll it takes for us to pass. we cape in gratitude
from behind the glass and blink dumbfounded
as the metropolitan disease contracts us. its practiced ease
sends us off in rhythm every day, down the piccadilly line,
in visible distress - the job long done once we are cold
and rocking on the tube.

                    the hooded eyes jump to and fro
between the passing windows, counting off, one two,
one two, just time to serve, just time to keep doing time,
for having got an in, another frozen soldier in a vast exhausted
army, marching at a trot, and forever on its toes, declutching
only in the outer travel zones – ain't no crumb of comfort
in the centre.

                    we keep it all untouched in there. we stay in step,
and never stop. it feels so good as long as we remain enlisted
in reaction. it takes so much from us, and all to lag behind.

escaped the source

this was how we partied back in the day of 1999:
beneath the vauxhall arches, on pounding feet,
the wall of bass resounding through our bodies.
we took coldharbour lane, we stole up brixton road,
through the little green, white faces sinister in shadow
and mine behind, just holding on, with eyes upon their feet,
letting them forge the way ahead, my eyes upon their backs,
hot breath upon my skinny neck, until we see the fridge,
and wait beneath the jutted chin to be let in, and probe
the anthem for a rush, a little desperate ecstasy, and bulldogs
swallowed for the joy of a mantra endlessly repeated,
and whirl beneath the bruising rig – and batten down
the hatches, and shoulder barge a way through the crowd,
in strobing light, all taut, relentlessly depleted
by the need to feel alright, and neck another one,
a loveless one to underscore the loneliness until

the GO GO GO, C'MON, LET'S 'AVE IT,

and drenched in sweat, a threaded ingress through the skin,
reaching in to fill my belly till i'm pregnant with it,
and not my world but their world, it in me and me exploding
in it, in all the brutish eyes upon me, in my hollow, grinning,
grim, triumphant rictus, all locked in on nothing, all locked
in upon the grave momentum of a savage beat down,
the vision of my own division clocked and copped
and in the darkness stowed away, my ticket on display
and in the morning read; the cruelty of a light
in which i find nothing to say, when coming down
to find myself still there and still one down, having passed
the test and having failed to do so, having been arrested
by the party line, still structured by unspoken privilege.

healthy gutted flora

how heavy sits the crown. those fuckers always stayed so clean.
the dirt got done beneath the water. the hurt stayed submarine
and brown. on the surface waved a probiotic and essential sneer,
the smell i smeared upon myself, the sniff that i could always hear
inside myself, all coiled up tight and hard in kind.
                                                        the arctic summers
we each woke intending to be seen. the years that i was welcomed in.
the jokes told loud enough for me to hear. we had the time to kill,
our only rush the need to drink the chill away. our cheers for disconnection.

the empties filled our tireless shells. the shelves restocked weekends
with bravado enough to move through every sullen street. no easy ride
for me. i tightened up in following quite faithfully the good old boys
impassive while i shuddered to be seen, a moth that found no place to rest
around their pale and lipless flames. the sweetest of performers.

they will never die. their lines are passed along at birth. they keep the rest
of us a little off, the mask kept in the act of slipping off, the task
to always need a little favour, a saviour and a shepherd, safe passage through
to port with broken gangplank hanging out, ready to be boarded. the rotten deck
will groan beneath their sterling boots. the cargo is bound up in the wreckage
of the hold, in the aching body strewn across the floor as if embalmed
to have to live that way, all frozen by that need of endless forward motion.

trickle down

i've got skill enough to bang a drum.
it's not the kind of sound to wrinkle crowns,
but will echo off a ceiling. i beat it down
to drive me on, in a move i moved upon myself
to force myself to move, to help me see myself
reflected up there in their sky replete with stars
and feel like one at last myself. this was the cost
of every blow i kept inside, where nothing scarred
or ever showed, kept alive enough to writhe beneath
the boots of those who never seemed to sweat themselves,
who never flinched beneath the whip but seemed equipped
to thrive instead beneath that spell, compelled to drive
it into every other.
                    they are the ones unsatisfied
with billions in dominion. they keep command
of the transaction, keep us understanding everything
as a transaction, hold the right and stay of the free enough
to go about assigning value. they do it all to make
a killing. they have the floor and so they march across it.
they spin the word to keep the tanks topped up.
they fuel the bastard engine, then turn it over, over time,
to turn you to the paradigm of inconsequential dying.
they'll have you run their fever till you burn the world
for them. each drop of blood, for them. no sweat.
they are a blood borne virus that divides and conquers
but regardless of desire. they only act to be conveyed
through time. they are assured of what they are to you.
what you are to them is clear in their articulate omission.

an instrumental roaming

i had it all but broke it up before i ever knew
i broke it up just to keep the score because division
is the rule and i learned the rule to learn to rule,
and ran that train upon myself to keep one down
to get one up, to privilege part to bury deep the other,
to leave it all the way back there on browning way,
to pass through the a4 grey, the great west road,
a growing void inside me, intent upon a more charismatic
post code, a more central demographic, a different style
of traffic and delay, a world away from how and slow
we lived in that disposable extremity. my life expectancy
went up with every mile; i turned and turned to take a turn
that could never come about. and then a turn too many,
and i was taken by my need to go, until i was forsaken,
left misshapen, stuck on blow, a shadow in a droning city,
a bitter statute in a vegetative body. i chipped away at stone
to mark the place the soldier fell. i was entombed in public
space, sealed right up behind a private line, in hell,
for none to ever see inside. and least of all myself.

i went in search of a home that i had never even seen.
there was a willful blindness in my yearning to survive.
i stepped upon the broken shards of a promise made
to stay asleep; i kept on stepping up to be the one
who followed in the wake of what was never spoken
of: all that tireless whom on what and where on whom
to remain unloved by the tireless march of their history.

all that carry on we carry

the quid pro quo of purity and right is always telling on itself:
it lends itself as aspiration and example - the jewel stays
on display, the gun stays trained abroad and in the city, centred,
to brutalize and exploit in both your adjacence and objection.

i had my function as a member of the company. i marched
beside my brutish mates; they loved a royal skinful. i learned
how i might kill myself because i was awful eager. i broke
my back to keep up with the deadly mission, a skillful student,
but one without the rank enough to catch the competition.

i never once got close enough to feel like i was close to even.

i got filled up with all the nerve of i don't need your shit no more.
i brought my shit instead, but all my shit was shit i'd brought
from home, all that foreignness, that absent feeling in the body,
that frozen alloy in the bone, the blood congealed and muscles
petrified, firm enough to step in stride and stay untouched in motion,
a distance always safe enough, that kept enough away, that killed
the feeling in all the ways i was ice inside and nothing even mattered.

we get transformed once we conform to fit the patriarchal mask.
the performance of our task is acting out and always in reaction
to what there ain't time nor reason for, nor profit in interrogating.
this is the duty we each pay. we give all the beauty of what arises
in us for the power of an anaesthetic drive, the insult thrown at us
that then becomes ours to use in turn, and don't it feel so good
to use, so good to sing that song as old as their recorded time.

i never guessed the history held inside. how far back was i
supposed to go when everything inside came from somewhere
that they had sought out to enlighten? i couldn't shake the guilty
burden, as if i owed myself to the load, for having had the chance
to cash out one time, just one time, and just a little some.

a drag ontology

the cause for which i gave myself was enough to fix me to a wall
on which you do not need to be above to push the other down,
but where you only need the will to push, and then you've got yourself
a little something, and all there is to do is push some shit around,
to take the space vacated and at a pace that leaves no place to return.

i left myself behind with nothing left to do but take off in the wake
of those i'd learned to kneel before in thrall, until i heard a call
from the end of my own tether, and from my lips fell the words:
you white bastard.

                        the response came in swinging. it hit me
in the ear, trickled down into the heart, where nothing can escape.

and everyone's a bastard here; each of us is only acting out of duty
to a fervent absent sense of ground. we're all so proud to have achieved
the art of a machine that takes evasive action and powers its own self down.

you kill it in your own self first, then kill it in another. you float above
your own damned head like frozen space debris. you're on collision course.
you're under orders and they're a killer: all that how to live, all acted out
for you to act it out again, to repeat the lesson to ensure that it's been learned,
to guarantee production will not stop, the senseless introduction of the weight
we carry in our foreign bodies, and all to pass it on, the culture of the kill.

fuckin paki

the moment becomes a beatdown, a broken spell
beneath which i will travel, but at a distance from the way
they tracked me with their heavy, wolffish eyes.
the vengeful moment of having nowhere left to hide,
my gut aversion to their touch, a bodied flight
and avid non-resistance. their neo-littoral pounce.
their frowning cyclone spinning on all sides that spun
away my breaking vessel. the fangtooth underbite
of grinning boots. my kicked in teeth upon the floor.

the blobfish gall of receding laughter. a pressure
in the body, a heavy yolk sac in the bones. a pinioned
gasp for air. the wish for all vibration to be stilled. the wish
to be allowed to go in silence, to make it somehow stop,
but it don't stop, not down there, in the flatline of protection.

the mouth of blood i spat out to smile. the palms i opened
as i mouthed the words that couldn't reach them nor obscure
the dirt now done, the dirt from which i'd always known i'd come,
the fuckin paki in my ears - go back to where you come from.

a shameful prick ran through my skein of self. a foul abyss
within my throat. my gut contracted to atomic mass. i gagged
and then it flowed, rolling to their feet in sorry genuflection.

the look they wore i knew too well for having always carried it
inside myself. i drifted out past the safety lines, a cow upended
on the wave, betrayed by the lament drawn out at just the sight
of land. the years spent placidly descending. the tired facade
of being afloat, exposed. the pretense of my worth. never worth
enough. there were too many of them - and not enough of me.

a gesture of acknowledgement

the penrose step of being both one up and down, first brown,
then man enough to understand exactly what it took to be a lover:
the trick of rule, the cunning of a fool who runs his empty lines
until he spies a chance to soothe his fear of missing out, his vapid
sense of scarcity, of having been excluded from some grand arena.
the dousing of a febrile need to be let in, to assert a sense of self.

we smudge the fine print at the bottom of the page and cross
the contract blindly. a season of goodwill to every man of violence,
whose claim to the throne lies with the stone inside his heart,
the granite affirmation of his wealth, his plastic health and empty
cheer, his central state forever self-confirming. we master proof
of rank to claim the badge devout. we give it all to make the kill,
to find ourselves contorted on the floor, beneath ourselves. we catch
those hands but dial it up and beat it on again. this is the father tongue.
we fall before that swollen bone for some relief from our own obstruction.
we seek a hole to fill, according to instruction, to kill the feeling worthless.

the triumph of one inside the other is in the boot held tight against a neck
that can never be let go. there is no sovereign without subject underfoot.
we're held this way in the constant tension of position: in a frozen study
of revenge, in punishment for all, caught in the act of always jumping
ship, ablaze in rage, while still, below, remaining locked up in the hold.

the get some blues

what i got was the need to look like i was somehow getting what i needed.
i whipped myself to stay upright, to feign the birthright ease and swagger
of the ones in active duty, with all their license of a lifetime's effort
to keep the windows closed. this is the essence of the privileged claim —
this violence in response to the endless call for ownership, the pistol grip
of one-upmanship. the brutal sermon is a liar. nothing can be owned.
the good might show up from time to time, but it can never stay for long.
every man must sign the contract; our hearts instructed not to file complaint,
not to burn with pain nor grieve our losses, just this guarantor of punishment.
the truth is in our being both the getter and the gotten. i betrayed myself in fear
of knowing i was the very hole through which i fell, my lonely out in the violence
i acted out and always on the inside, for never having learned my problems
stemmed from having learned, at the beginning, that what i lacked was value.

toothpaste ghost line

every modern birth has both an inherited and an inherent value.
the lesson of my own worth, compounded by the english one,
was first taught me by the shadow of a man upon the edges
of perception, a man who left me reacting to the threat of new rejection,
compelling me to leave the world before it could ever get there first.

the best thing about addiction is that when the hardest shit goes down,
you frown and shrug then go get fucked like it don't mean a thing.

i encountered him again in the corridors of a job: a strange, familiar
face, all faded parchment creased around the eyes, a private smile
that wavered in between indifference and amusement, a line
of dried-up toothpaste running from the corner of the mouth;
some ashen, ghostly mirror reflecting things i'd never seen before.
he was so beaten up and grey that i couldn't help but smile.

a weightless and unfeeling hand reached out to straighten up his tie.

the first and fiercest hate i'd always reserved for my own self.
i took all meaning from an infant's understanding of responsibility,
the nascent and non-verbal knowing that i had been the wrong.

this is how it goes when you are young: you soak it up inside,
then pull yourself apart. you watch yourself depart, then carry
on, and never dare to turn around to see the one you left behind.

not once did anybody say to me: retrace your steps, young man.
not once did anybody say to me: this isn't yours to carry.

my cells betrayed a care i couldn't yet begin to fathom.
a bastard quiver in the chest and all suffering forgotten.
imprinting really does begin before you ever breathe.

the presence of his absence in my body was a game
of one truth and three essential lies, my grief and anger
and my guilt, the loudest room i'd never heard myself
inside. instead i scanned his face to note the ways the rent
was made. i traded drinking time for scant regard.
i watched that silent curl until i couldn't take no more,
for the only thing it ever seemed to say to me, was this:
now here's the kicker, kid, but let's never talk about it.

the two of us were entwined in bloody matter,
but he declined my cut from his own flank,
abandoned me to bleed out on the platter,
and i reeled for having been discarded.
pulling rank, i sealed it up. this is the learning
of the modern age: the myriad ways to disengage
from your own self.
                              this is the lowly passage
that i've navigated, the less than feeling leading
me in every wrong direction. this is a wide shot
of the lonely years i wound around myself
like a frozen carousel. now i have unlearned
each line, and though it's taken me some time
i have been doing what i can. here is what i've made
of it: my disenfranchised burn, an oceanic suture.
i've warmed to every aching morning i squirmed
beneath the brine. i'm feeling my way back
through how i broke along the spinal ridge to grow,
rock solid, entrenched inside the rent, to subside unseen.

this is the blow that i now feel, the harnessed plow
of something that once split, the cost i paid to find myself
here in the tear of that redacted and ahistorical transaction.

the cop out by the fence that lines the yard

a feast of food for thought in seeing:
the eyes, the channels to the mind,
the images withheld in time behind
an inside shake, inside this burning
skin and how i couldn't say a word.

the same strange fever dream arose,
a choking field, a watching shadow:
the urge to fly away. the need to flee
and the blissful anguish of having fallen,
wide awake, insistent on forgetting.

the seed of doubt once sown contracts
us all to form around a void of feeling.
we go to work obliged to land that void
on one another. i went out like a man,
but i was mostly not a man. how everybody
seems to be, all bodied by that sleepy draught;
all blood retained to boil abreast for reason
of our unguessed rage - to act it out instead,
to quell the danger understood as a violent
or destructive thing.

                        to never know its beauty.

this is the holding pattern of our protection:
the duty to deny, the fractal pattern a buried turn
held deep inside a gravid body. we keep it safe
from everyone except ourselves. it's just too hard
to see beyond the earnestness of all our wanting
to abscond from our own selves. it's just too hard
to mourn all that we've done to never change a thing.

the unfree versus

the stove got hot just one time and was kept
in mind as being hot forever. the system built itself
from that first time to make a stranger of the self.

they call it lost in thought for a reason, the reason being
our need to look up to the frontal lobe in awe, to keep
in mind the line that defines it as the lowest ceiling;
to keep me here above, and me down here, below,
asundered, an x against the question y, a little plot
of feeling gone awry, an illegality - the wave of correlation
describing no relation but the distance between me and reality.

please hold. i think i'm on the other line. let me put
you through. the ringer sounds like you, if a little older.

no one dreams of ending up a piece of shattered glass.
but here we are, all scuttling past like there were none
transgressed and never a transgressor. every window's
boarded up and we're just peeking through, forever,
always tense, kept on guard against transgression,
until it comes and we hold it off, feeling in our hands
held overhead as if we are engineered to be offhanded:
the wave gets dealt with and redacted, unhanded
by the strongest hand to hand it off somewhere.

it goes unfelt that way. it stays unsaid and we part ways,
inoculated in all the ways that we have learned to disappear.
so off we go in search of cure, as if the search itself
could be the cure, as if there were a cure or any ailment
but this holding off the rise that builds inside us as a wave
and swells with promises to pass - but stays forever cresting,
pearled in frost, withheld, held off, hold back, hold out, forget it.

this is the unconscious reaction that dams the tributary up.
everything determined by anxiety, bearing arms against our being
caught unarmed again beneath the ugly weight of memory.
we keep ourselves at arm's length, deprived of our felt sense
in preference for a glassy commonality, the painless way
we have of suffering without feeling.

                                        i had the sensuality
of a youthful soldier's corpse. i gave my arms; they bore,
disarming - hurt held far enough away i could give it just enough
to seem to give it up sometimes.
                                        it got hard to breathe, sometimes,
for all that i could never feel, for the killing of the daily quota,
the lightning burn, the lyric torn from my clenched tight, my fight
for air, the fight to keep my fight forever on the down low, my voice
denied its natural range to wander, these sorry little bird-like bones
that held the wave after wave as if to preserve the sense of somehow being
alright; these little digital hooks confined to slave for hypnotizing
a held body in its endless quest for safety. the absence of any safety
or repose in always serving the quest to douse and soothe the fire
in the eternal question of living. these shaky little bone hooks,
holding fast the wave above my head as if they could forever.

you do though don't you though

the cop will pull you up. the boss will ask you over.
the voices of erasure always press on first one part
and then another. their pressing need to do it over,
to do the move that moves between us, holding down,
and keeping dumb, unable to attend to what arose
about the one about whom it arose. the rote recital
of the habit of division. but resistance has to be forgiven.
the war was fought to win the right to send the self away.
the war was always mine. it's always been internal.
the system learned for me to be forgotten, held behind
the dam inside, the damn shame of i am, i know: divided,
stasis in the constant recapitulation of a patriarch's mis-giving.

lesson learned

the system had me on my knees in fear of one day
being received and judged and summarily discarded.
i copped the plea, took the offered deal of servitude
in lieu of safety and no change then in the world.
and it was me that abandoned me, the lonely doing
doer. perhaps it was required to know my difference
better, to know the ways that i will crush the seed
then rush in to defend it. this cost that i have paid
will never be repaid. it may not even be acknowledged,
except by me, alone. i know enough to know myself
what happened, now: the ways i flinched when the performers
read their lines, the ways the tremor overwhelms and i take
myself away, trapped in the hold behind a frozen smile,
a problem not to be resolved, the cop out on patrol,
the one who always sees me coming, grabs my arms
and marches me away from the scene so fast i never see
who i am leaving there, behind. who's waiting there for me.
i was slow in noting the system threatened by my noting.

process singh / memory kaur

the eyes of memory hold the rent long overdue; what do you do
when memory cannot take you there and none who know themselves
will guide you on the way? you work with what you have. you scan
the faded photographs. you sketch a timeline from the faces you once
wore, hang out inside your earliest recall to try to feel what sent
you reeling. you feel what you can feel. and then you go from there.

a child is just the overlapping dance upon a wall of grainy shadows
thrown by random candles. i was waiting in a lot, the backseat of a car
with no idea why we were there, so unprepared to see the man come
stalking across the lot to me. she fled as he approached, left me alone
with my panicked wait for words that would not come. my plea a whine
for her to save me from this tip toe, lie low, no show mother-fucker,
this braggadocio of care but just for number one. this man for whom
i'd been the practice run, and easily forgotten.
                                         i watched him roll
up to the window. he put his hand upon the roof, spoke down
to the breach, then reached inside for me. i tensed and warped away.
hid in my arms, the project underground held tight enough to break
the bone between the muscle. i breathed it in but never let it go.
the word caught in my throat, a sound i could not make - a yes,
for having once belonged to him, for his having once been mine.
i kept it all inside. i pushed it down the throat, back down to acid,
counted out my frozen breath and watched behind a throbbing veil:
the dimming glare of haloed daylight, a ticking clock corroding
on a distant, heavy shelf. the black corona of the closing frame.
until he left, again. and i got stuck that way.
                                         i'd failed to reattach.
it wasn't safe for me. how could it ever be? he hadn't once been mine.
the choice was never mine to make. and yet they'd put it all on me.

she watched him go and then relaxed and carried on as ever. the only choice
i got to make was how to frame what had happened. so i copped the blame
for what i couldn't choose for them. i split that day, for having silenced,
for having understood myself as the reason for his absence, the reason
for her frozen keen: the syllabi they wrote for me, the way i learned my lesson.
and now the course is run. and this is where it ends. we all get done somehow.
a little less for some, a little more for others. that's just how it goes. look
it up sometime, it's written in the sky. slow it down. it sounds a lot like rain.

separation anxiety

defeat shook me awake. i found myself
trapped in a viscous web, held down
by the morbid drag of newfound weight.
a stunned detachment. kept in suspension:
my sudden apprehension of a distance
i would never cover, for being covered
in the sticky repetition of a deed long done.
a failure of reporting back, for having gone
and kept on going then to find my body
had become an ancient, out of date receiver
- of the word of the makers and educators
of the law, the reason i wore the face of war
inside, the battle i fought to deny all genuine
reaction, the mute indictment of a bag left
unattended on the tube - the mindless crowd
which shooed me down the line and cast me off
the platform, the means by which i had been overrun,
the work of progress, the endless struggle against
the self - the violence of commuting. the need
to suck in air.

the startle of relief i felt
one day when the gears ground to a halt.
the shock. the echoed call of pain that came
from deep within the heart's hydraulic press,
long since shut down by the ice inside the vein,
to live a life through lonely, knowing no one cared
what i had seen when i was first in line.
a warning gleaming in the eyes to never get
too close. the anxious way a user gets in company,
in expectation of remand, desirous of sole custody,
trapped in the moment with the law reflecting back
and such a long time coming. there is no comfort
in the fear of being seen, the tireless croon inside the ear,
a ghost ship scene played out in time, a hanging wall
of mist from which you find yourself repeatedly emerging.

there was a blinding flash inside the frame, a nearby crack, an echoed other, and the shutters were thrown open wide to find that blown through them came a wind that burned the skin of its rabid urge to leave, and yes, too late, for now the frame was gone, and there at last was i, and for a single flashing moment i was aware that somewhere down the line i had become divorced from my existence.

death, a valley and you lie in it

you can hear it in the echo of the fearless valley, the unlit passage
underground, a tireless whispered now and now and now and now,
and as the floorboards sway beneath your feet you think, to yourself,
yeah, that's the way, that's all the way i'm in it - but we ain't met
before and we sure as hell ain't meeting now, 'cause how's a self
inside it go again. no, we don't get to go again. we go
with all the pressure of our practiced metropolitan desires,
the always moments of our single rareness, split in every second
and never stopped to reconvene in wonder at the sight
of what comes to us in defeat, those precious teargas moments
when we cannot deny the lie of all security, the knowledge we are
out here, quite alone, defenceless, pushed out through the frame to fall,
all formless, damned to fail to land, preformed to curve around
and hand the self back in, in the end, a boomerang, the hardest stake
that we all get to carve. the impact of it driving in makes one from two,
unscarred despite it all and recombined, returned once we are gone
from sight, and that's alright, 'cause ain't no backing out now. we're
on the ride and inching forward with the night sky in our eyes. let's trawl
for light and let these words catch nothing in our hearts but love.

the genogram

the first that anybody ought to say is, yeah, shit happens to us all. it happens
to each of us when we are young and open, when we are pure devotion
in another's hands, in hands that reach within us and stay there for a lifetime.

it doesn't matter whose. it only matters that it happens. it isn't said enough.

so here we are, with every chance to apprehend the ways we got so rigid -
the moments we were caught in time like an impala wandered from the herd
becomes alerted to a closing cheetah, the passing seconds counting out
the same belief that we've been caught, in the breach, and are clinging on to time
as it wraps itself around us, as it traps us in our circling breath and threads
us through the pulse of every falling hourglass grain of sand that links
each moment to the next and pulls us taut between them.
                                                      for every child
that cries and sees that no one comes no matter how they cry will swallow
what they feel and turn it in upon themselves. they'll grow the space between
their newly silent tremors and wait for an exhausted sigh to carry to them
on the wind.

            we wait though wired to rush, kept in demand of constant action.
we carry out our one command, to carry on in perpetual reaction. we double-cross
ourselves. we toss ourselves out overboard. we dive and scramble to affix
the masks we learn to wear as custom to our faces, but they don't fit so well.
we each have skill enough to send ourselves to sleep. we learn to keep the fitful
nightmare running. we leave behind the one who stumbled out of time,
that distant kin transmitting over light years all their faint report of feeling.

can't stop, be leaving

leaving is a full-on, full-time occupation,
a full tide always turning. there's no time
to take the times insurgent dive, to stop
the braiding of the self in time or weep
for ever having been enmeshed in fervent,
fraught reaction. the learned system
is a yawning need to censor what comes
up, and a warning always heeded. alarmed,
we stay defended. we reprehend ourselves
for ever risking our own freedom. beaten
down by every thought, the catechism
of a bitter tiding, a distance far too great,
an understanding that once came in
through the ears and travelled down,
to the heart, to where the lesson lives.

we haunt ourselves inside our heads.
we are a knowing web that learned
to spin itself and watch it being spun.
we leave for work to work to leave
a fortress without exit. the concrete
poured will set. the dust kicked up
by endless daily labour settles to reveal
the obstacle only taller than before.
we settle there, trapped behind the tacit cord
pulled taut so as not to feel ourselves
inside the binding, so as not to ever come
undone but stay forever in the thing that built
itself, around itself, and for its own protection.

two nil to them

the system keeps its promise.
there is a safety in the stitching
of every single bitter moment
in a foggy, shrouded arras,
in being both the endless torrent
and the dusty, wayward scribe,
in being the ramparts and the throne,
the archer and the arrow sticking
out the sun-dried leather body.

the choice of being either the getter
or the gotten is no choice at all.
i made it just so i could have it made;
i worked to stuff and frame a living
thing and fix it to the wall.
i flailed against the web
in which it was impressed on me
to hold myself. i took so long to fall.
but everything must fall: everything
we lose in all the distance we create.

amateur dramatics

this is the phantom of an afterthought, the dull description
of a faint chalk outline drawn when something living thought
a thought and began to fade away. this is a move like ants that crawl
out from the secret darkness of a crack inside a wall to reach
the reckoned safety of another. this is the dread and ceaseless march
by which i've always been entranced. the system first commands
the move and then observes the troop go by. i fail to see where one
begins or where the other ends. i can't discern the thing they bear aloft,
the strange dark mass around which i have somehow formed. i understand
this mass as being carried by a convoy guard. i understand this mass
as being passed along a static line. my overwhelming need is to prevent
suspicion of any movement in the mass itself. it remains transported
in this frozen state. all movement is restrained to just the thought of how
the movement moves. the system acts to never know the name
of what it keeps, constantly departing. this is what i have learned,
of performance: this endless rabid pacing back and forth from one side
to the other of a shadowed stage. we scramble fervently to catcall
the empty space in which we are convinced that we were standing.
we stay in motion so as not to break the illusion of performance on the stage.
we never stop to peer out at the empty house for which we all perform.

there is no self here in the world as hard to do as doing nothing to ourselves.

the jack knife

this sense of always being on the verge of running out
as if you need to be elsewhere. this sense of needing to be
far enough away from here that no one will ever see you.
this sense of making sense of the fact that this is what
you've been fighting for: to never do what you must do
but look as if you do. this sense of having been divided
with a bounty on your head. this sense of having had to force
yourself to keep yourself in line, but never with yourself,
of having had to pay this price but for your own protection.
this othering device that keeps you going in the way of what
you did must have been something really wrong. this song
that you've been singing all your days, this burning knife
that cauterized each crucial valve, this salve that numbs
you not for having done some wrong but for having learned
you were the wrong, and having turned against yourself.

self-deprivation

i made a statue of my self and placed a wreath to me beneath it.
i interred the lesson learned, cursed out an undisclosed lament,
the sublimation of my intent to live up to the name i was given,
a pact i made to keep on doing what they did as proof of my lack
of value.

       the crime rate starts increasing once the jail is built. the walls
create a vacuum. they suck you in to fill them up. you live your life
accosted. you learn to pay no mind at all as every blow keeps landing.

framing carpentry

that's a real good wall, the kind that holds its own.
hidden in it are instructions. you've been reading
them all your life. they keep you busy winding on
just like a spooled cassette, always there, recorded,
sometimes loud, and sometimes whisper quiet,
and other times when you are playing dead
though you're still there, still seeking out the answer
to the tragic question, how you might keep on doing what
you do, all you have ever done, all you have ever wanted
to achieve: the reason for your every action. the reason
you can't grieve. the reason you can't hold your reason
to your heart, the heart you'll never know as long as you
identify with what keeps you from your answer, with what
does not seek an answer, not loud nor whisper quiet,
with what is always playing dead, the ghost that doesn't want
to die, the system that insists on being alive in everything you do,
that answers every question with itself, everything it knows
on foundations built from all the history you've accrued,
each brick placed carefully in time to form a monument
to all the work you did to never dwell on what had formed,
to never read the fine print at the bottom of the contract
commanding you to build these walls around yourself,
to stay locked up inside your head, stay hard at work
and always out of courage, fearful, driven, dreaming
of the day that you'll down tools and open up the windows,
which you will never do, 'cause you were made to try.

the stage has long been set for you: the body has become a cage in which you are required to disengage from every painful feeling. you disavow your reality; you writhe and squirm each day instead beneath the dirty light refracted through the prism of experience, the spectrum of your need to seek escape from hidden wounds projected on the prison walls, entrained within a greying body playing dead upon a silent gurney. you're held in tension, stiff and numb, a bed within the muscle. it's such a heavy, bitter turn, but memory burns its shield. it burns itself, to feel the split and so, to let it heal, so you will know the privileged part that works to never know itself or ever feel what has been kept unconscious in the hold. the ever undisclosed. that nameless weight inside.

a tragic seed

everything that you've accrued in living is commandeered
as capital for the system to make a killing. all its wealth
is in the history kept alive inside the body, all the memory
held in tension in the flesh to make it stiff and numb. all our
living mean, our loathsome, grave, conditioned fate,
to end up in the aging cell. there's no escaping a lifetime's
doing for having once been overwhelmed. we are compelled
to live apart inside the head for having once been given grounds
to think that this was how to live.
                                    for trauma is a fact of life
and no one can avoid it. out in the wild they shake it off,
but here we're stuck inside it, held hostage to the rent,
contorted and malformed prisoners of old responses locked
away, old, lost objections to some trespass once suppressed,
distorting what we think, reporting only distance from the feeling
of the moments when we found ourselves unable to respond,
the moments when we held ourselves in tight defeat and twisted
and deformed, the moments still occurring in us like new wounds
from which we go on twisting and deforming. we hold on tightly
to ourselves in this continual reaction. the system in us learned
from all the system in the world, to work to make it last a lifetime
and never question just how long a lifetime ought to be endured.

the dog bounced off the wheel

each arid moment has a surface calm
but buried in it lies a trampled fencepost
bearing markings of a boundary line.
you get however many years you get
to unearth it and see it stood upright again,
but are prevented from beginning
by the anguish of your reaction. you run
yourself into the ground to stay in place
and just as long as you remember.
this is the way we have of living mean,
the means test of our forgetting everything
that ever happened to us, our never once
forgetting, our holding all those moments
close enough to live them over and over again.

but nothing here is lost. the fallen will arise
again; the beaten soldier stirs once more
in the aftermath of battle, the ghost
compelled to writhe on history's field
in acquiescence to the one command,
that comes and goes behind the wire a separate
person in the end, a part of all they did
to you, and even if you never knew, but waited,
rigid, through it all, convinced that nothing
happened. you'll be required to open.
something here will open you, by opening up
itself to you, by giving itself to receive you.
this is the trick that turns outside of time. the gift
provided in it. all your struggle is given to you
for you to know yourself, for you to journey back
through time, and ain't no place else to go but back -
to the source of every feeling. there ain't nothing else
for you to know and no other way to know it.

my head turned all the way around

we play defense on every thrust
but let the system have its way.
we're distantly retained in hope
that it might somehow be exhausted.

we stay numb enough to disappear;
we're nothing in the rear view
showing - the world revolves this way,
with nothing knowing of the ways
that we are each impaired to do,
and so imbued we might as well
you know, if only for protection.

we are descending, bluff, without affection
as the building grows around us slow.
each passing floor is why i always felt
one down, dejected, automatically
divested, brick by brick, of everything
i was. this is how it was. condolences
do not redact the losses. none of this
was mine to choose. i was meant
to forget the way my pieces go together.

shell branded dungarees

we aren't intended to prevail. no matter
how we learn to limit how we touch the life
inside us, how we poke so absent-mindedly
at all the pressure points of those beside us,
how we push or pull at one another to spin
our little threads of fantasy – we'll never once
prevail. but we can't stop the bloody effort.
we keep on going endlessly. how little rest
we are allowed, as if the stars alone appear
familiar.

       the whispered now became too loud;
the breath that beckoned me return to you
invoked my need to hold myself, but tenderly.
it rendered me a smile arisen from each blurry
image come to mind, to leave the steps away
untaken, with care enough at last for care itself,
the care to come and go a self; not to fight it,
but to hold my heart and let the world unite us.

twenty twenty

i've been six foot one apart from you
for more than thirty years. i was unprepared
to witness the uncreated and unbroken
movement of you entered into. i departed
time and time again, unseen, behind the line,
reacting to the notion you were never mine,
that what you'd felt i could not bear. i bore
the world instead, that smiling, caustic cruelty,
that exhausted politic, that killing for an overhead,
that kick directed down.

                    and then i heard you cry.
a sound composed not of seconds nor the silence
in-between but of a montage of the pieces i was not
allowed to feel. the pieces held in place, your
wilfulness at last restored, your little head at rest
upon my shoulder, your glowing face pressed
in my neck. your breath a puzzle to be solved,
your pieces of performance that i held: the feeling
that the war was over - for i could see myself at last,
and while nothing here will bring the stage set down,
no bolt of lightning will lay it bare and i remain
here with the set still standing, with no dramatic thing
occurring, now you and i are together in the warmest
correspondence. and all i hope is that we pass away
the way of nothing left to do, but hold you in my love.

a stigmatic resolution

to be exhausted by the unrecorded ebb and flow
of the inexhaustive movement means to give up
all the struggle with the struggle, to take the beat
that we are given, the little patch we keep in order,
the border we patrol, and there refuse to march,
no hypervigilante.

                that essential work ain't mine.

the moment of refusal is an end to all the need
to get inside. the struggle with the struggle
ends up patently absurd. you see how you will lose
both pulse and breath that way. you stay adjunct,
kept always extra, incomplete, turned inside out,
retained in disconnection, maintaining the monolithic
block, the lie those pale intruders sold to you to seed
their kill on your unceded hinterland.

                       let's move
in both directions at one time. detachment
isn't cold and lonely if we move that way
together. i am the one who holds and i am
the one being held. the seal is broken and we gaze
both ways in love of attachment and detachment.

this is how the world was made; the one divided
from itself to feel itself a world. this is the move begun
by all i feel for all that i've remembered. it hurts
to know how far i went. the system never wanted me
to come to this but the native pattern doesn't care
for any such resistance. there is no need to disappear.

you cry. that's what you do

there is a path the world beats into us. we march
in service of a system created in naïve response
to the hardest question asked of us. the system
doesn't wish to see it be resolved but seeks to keep
it always asked. this engine fuels our flight – the path
of most resistance – all momentum engineered
by our insistence on this holding tight to the box
we once shut closed so none could see inside it.

nothing would be the same again if we were to pry
it open, for then there'd always be this opening,
this cycle of the moment out there on the verge
from which for us to leap, in order to return.
but always is a step too far for us. we do all
that we do to not do that. instead we fight to pass.

                    but it's alright to try and make a little space inside,
                    if only for a wild and sideways glance at the montage
                    of a perfect one and an imperfect other. the ebb
                    and flow between these ghostly poles is the system
                    come undone inside the teargas moment of the feeling
                    of the movement of the self as you step off from the path
                    to love yourself and cease to leave yourself behind.

back up, back up, back up, back up

a buried seed is filled with the need to free itself,
but there's no way to free yourself from time,
no way out that strange stenosis wrapped around
the painful knowledge that you keep inside,
remote, cerebral, so as not to emote nor integrate,
to never grieve bereavals. ain't nothing free enough
to free itself. we're only free enough to pay the cost
as every crisis moves beneath the crushing burden.

you move through time with what you've learned
and all you've learned you had to learn so you could learn
unlearning and become a part of nature once again. you
are a casing made to shatter, a native shoot unwinding
through the dirt to find the sun and once begun
it's inescapable - the return to antimatter. its bidden
by itself, toward itself. it comes on a wave that roars
toward us across the darkest ocean. but we will hold
it up, that soaring wall of frozen glass, held high above
our heads, as if to keep it there forever, though it is sure
to crash down in the end and take us back whence
it has come. it doesn't matter if we hold out to the end.
it doesn't matter if we never move an inch but prove
that we have strength enough to close our hearts to the fact
of our ever having fought, or fled, or ever having frozen.

no one here is further on and none are being left behind.
all labour is the project of projection, all slow-motion
and a learned direction. we can know no other. we suffer
every breath in hope of yet another: the frozen mechanism
of our knowing props us up - we watch but never map
the ways in which we are always taken. we make a breathless
leap of our surveillance, a holy claim to nothing. the absence

of recording doesn't mean a thing. there's nothing here to gain,
no capital to be accrued, no power nor transcendence,
just what remains by nature useless to ambition
and every purpose we devise. when we talk about it
something like a cornered rat runs through the shadows
of our minds so fast we find we cannot tell ourselves a thing.
this isn't work that thought can do. the doing is a feeling.

a chariot still travels

it's a trip that every single effort i ever made
amounted in the end to naught. it's a gift, i guess -
one bought and processed and which shipped
regardless how i paid. the war was always fought
for the single purpose of my inevitable surrender.
this was the end of all that time i spent alone,
outside myself - an end i couldn't bring about.
all i ever sought to bring about was my perpetual
departure, to never get somewhere.

                          i got there
in the end. i've been unarmed by battle. i'll fight
when called to fight, but not to prove myself again.
i carry my own self upon the way, so now i go
with care. there are no false directions. the war
around me rages still, and so i keep my arrow
ready, ever notched, vibrating in the bow.
i watch for friend the same as foe and foe
the same as friend. when i hear the call to let my arrow
fly, i watch the finger on the string release itself,
i watch the work be done, and then forget it all.
now i remember you, beloved. the two of us
watch as the hand restrings the arrow. once i chose
to push or pull and never moved a thing.
now i choose to be moved instead. this is the nature
of decision, noncombatant, fighting to the end,
if only to begin again, with you here in my arms.

a promise kept; a promise keeper

this is how it works: the system born of pain contains
your mind to intertwine the sound that you once made
when drowning with all that you learned to do to never hear
that sound again and everything you learn to do becomes
the thing on which it carries itself away. but the cognate
of cognition and emotion can override this cycle of reaction.
integration is the function with which to oppose the system working
over time. what is the worth of your essential work? the noise
of all that you must do? there's only ever less for you to do
to not be overlooked by your own self, to not let expectation
cloud your thought and return all defenses back to the vast
unspoken. you needn't heed the endless warnings to escape.
let's take the time's insurgent dive instead. let's divest ourselves
from the drive behind that grave construction. let's give no
service any more to that direction but instead let every act become
a new refusal of that system. we've been beholden for too long.
the anxious warnings carry an unintended communique of freedom
from carceral protection. the walls we each have made do not need to hold
us. i have me in my arms now, in joy and love of such responsibility.
there is no trick to it, no penance first to serve, no custom to observe,
no altar to bow down before nor gift of alms to place upon it. i'm here
with me and want to stay until the end, with all the mystery of my feeling
touched where expectation ends and we are free to move as one,
in all the ways we move when we are one, unbodied, epistemic groove.

harbinger dhoom

i turned as if through time, went back to agriculture,
turned my martialed forces back to tillage and to care,
to irrigate the soil and grow new forms, without shame
at the unexpected sight of my defeated soldier turning
back to work the land. i sweat beneath the same sun still.
i worked the soil that held the child inside. i bodied my precious
difference. i put the self at tireless service of that growing edge.
i laboured without yoke and for an end i could never bring about.
there is no way to choose to raise not one defence against this
always being carried. there is no greater threat to us than this:
the horror of our lines all having been pre-written, the panic
of a human life with nothing left to do but love the self.
and now i'm learning to, the world appears to me brand new,
and what a world that it could be if all of us were able to.

the illusion of a gun

all the memories buried in the muscle cannot stay for long:
no absences interred inside the body there belong, nothing
i believed that i had done could be so wrong that you deserved
to be forgotten. no fruit of feeling ought be judged as ripe
or rotten, yet thought is trained to be the cop out on the beat,
the maker of the law and educator of it, and all because the hand
that picks the fruit must pass unseen. but still the body knows
enough: it feels that touch and watches as the wheel revolves.

this is the movement of its love. the duty of momentum is a turn
that turns itself but always with affection. it turns through feeling
and pre-verbal sound, with no other duty but a duty to itself,
duty in the lonesome breath's atomic charge in every cell,
the hushed procession of the endless little blows, in each exhale
exploding every thought - and question of command.
                                                    i occupy
my post to leave it empty of disdain; i fill it all for you, beloved.
you are my one command. i demand no more than this from me:
to give myself what i did not receive - the reason for the ache
in every moment i stood out on the verge with my wired eyes
sustained only by the invisible horizon, all feeling distant in my body,
my mind a cage that worked to silence all the wonder of my birth.
now judgement's ashes lie untouched, as on a winter morning.

bhakti life

we all get bodied in accordance with the rhythm
of the beat down that we first receive. we keep it
down inside our beating sense machines, our moving
parts a moving part in an immense machine, a universal
dance of soft machines, all unbodied till the war is lost
and we appear at rest, six foot down, for having passed
the test of the system's will to never question how we feel
until it is too late. the system knows enough to see us coming:
it keeps us going, every second stayed, eternally expended
and perpetually unused - like nothing done by nothing.

the hardest thing is to go without the ontoepistemic
scope of you - your reason for having come when we go
so soon. so i am going to try and keep this scene inside
my head, this vision of us two, because division is a dream,
and what is one divided but a part of what it is apart from,
if still in touch while yet untouched? i never touched it
till the need to keep accruing gave up on itself. echoes
still remain - the need to keep on feeling nothing, all systemic
and created by itself to keep itself forever distant from itself,
to only ever enter into what it has to do - which is holding
off the only thing that it can know, that it can never let be
known, because it's how you feel. but i can feel you now,
and from this verge i will be carried, and carry me myself.
you are my perfect circle. and you are always thus, beloved.

the radcliffe line

let me let you off the hook off, then. everybody here
was sent away from themselves to learn for their selves
to always happen to themselves. this is the way it goes:
so who's to say who's had it worse? well some are told
that it should not have been allowed to ever happen,
while others find that when it does it is a thing no law
forbids and that the world was glad to witness, nodding,
laughing as it watched. so who's to say who's had it worse?
well, okay. while it will happen to everybody in some way,
it sure will hit us different. some get run right through.
they scream and scream, and everybody hears them scream,
but almost everybody has been drilled to hear nothing
and pass it on. while many drill themselves. they bear the cut
as if they ought not speak themselves, as if they are not worth
the mention, as if the worst thing they could do is make trouble
for the killers, so lie awake at night doubting everything
that they have lived. they lose the right to speak. too many
lose the right to breathe. and others keep their innocence
maintained, speaking in voices of erasure, their voices deadly
smooth, like euthanasia, lucky as they go, denying everything
that happened.
                and if, as they hold, nothing really happened; if
the worst was just our being born – well okay, it is enough.
the killers then repeat the lesson we first learn when rent from one
to somehow be another. this is the pain of stunned partition,
the bitter shut-in moment of the brand-new heart.
                                                    but, remember:
it doesn't stay that way for long. we open up the hold inside, alone.
we scream ourselves into the world, anew. i will keep these ears
alive, these channels to the heart, through which the music moves.

protection under lotus feet

it's transformative to perform the apperceptive tactic of letting yourself be taken. take the tree that waited all those empty sidewalk years for me to see it bend its skinny branches to my dusty window. when i finally noticed i reached to interweave my freezing fingers with its trembling leaves, as if i might atone, and so we held our hands like that each morning for two good years, in the dawn, my being held inside the tree, a gentle seeing of internal eyes, a tacit listening to music in its bark and sap and amber; a moving with and through the phloem and the xylem in its cells.

there was this tenderness of becoming the self-same life that moved in it that moved in me and moved me then to cease my moving, that made me hold instead to it alone, for it to know itself in me and only as a friend; for us to come to one another, but as a conduit, to let the life inside us touch itself and let itself be touched. we two were one made one again in contact and made for that alone. we wound around ourselves in kindness and the music of the dancing leaves.

i had to close my eyes to see. there was this difficulty in the common channel to the mind. it was hard to see beyond the stem by which i was attached, to where i fell: the difficulty in my being rooted and in seeing everything alive. this difficulty stemmed from my desire to stay alive and see ahead eternally. the call came in through the ear instead, to lead the way in love of word and song and breath, and passed through every leaf and branch and bark and ring, and all the unseen scheming roots beneath. through everything that passed in-between, therein - the breath that does all things, but only does itself. the breath that does all things, and does it all with feeling.

there is a movement always rushing off to where i'll never know and will never see arriving. there is a one that does not force itself but moves upon my skin as if it were its own. it moves as if it's nothing, as if it doesn't know itself or even what it's doing. it moves as if it is an ocean, like one that knows no up or down but carries its own self back to itself, all by itself, the great and small alike.

the space between us two is nothing more than this: the childlike difficulty i must share with you in this, the epistemic season of a wind that carries every leaf with care back to the ground without ever being asked.

refuse the racket

can we at least then agree that something happened here?
everybody goes away - and keeps on going in that way
with everything inside them, all that trembling breath
withheld, that shaking project of the tide which threatened
once to overwhelm them, that overcame them once to leave
them then in no way inclined to come back to their selves,
unconscious of what happened in a world that watched
it happen and then carried on without them, left on the margins
of appeal without a way to leap back from that white-hot flame,
with backs against the wall. the mechanism of the rent for one
and never for the other.
                    we're all picked off at birth and put to sleep,
but not to dream. it's so hard to stay up through the night,
awaiting light enough to fight back for a life you know is moments
from its end. you stay unheard as long as you endure. you stay
assured when you know not to fight when called to fight, to never
let refusal sound to ground yourself when they are acting out.

how long can we stay numb and silent as the killers do us in?

let's not be so porous. let us be clear on what is ours, and what
was never ours to take. i was so easily disposed of. i have learned
to give myself what i never once received. i am my father now.
i hold myself in my own arms and feel such love to see me there.
my eyes reflect the value of the newborn feeling sense, a pure
devotion to experience: another chance to leap in every breath.

in every ban

there was a devastation in the way i asked her to tell me about poetry.
then, the simple way she said: first you strip the flesh off from the bone,
and then you scream. i held her in such high esteem but couldn't hold myself
that way. each line was wrong and throwaway. i was intransigent if truth be
told, still controlled inside by what i'd learned of absent men and care.
once it took inside i never felt alright enough again to feel alright again.
i get it now, i guess. there ain't no way for you to get it till it's given itself
to you, then you know you had it all along. then the scream comes after,
an outburst of verse intended to recant, a rant, recalcitrant and full of longing
for all that once belonged to you, the grief of your lost love for you,
the twinkle in your eyes as your infant cries resolved into laughter.

this is a brand-new sound resounding on the intercom, a revolution in stereo,
an improvised, staccato moment that revolves around the beauty of a faded
photograph, the image reel of my younger self come to mind again, arisen
as a limbic sign, a temporal comeback, the payback for the absent sad sack
and the lack he left behind, the chair he never occupied, the lifelong rupture
now repaired. that regulator somehow purged, that grim-faced judge who othered
and refused, recused. i've been offered immunity from that implacable detention.
that always off inside has been located and i'm no longer swayed, but entered;
the sense of having been enough, of feeling free enough at last to give what
was not received. two parts freshly braided along the intact line between us.
we lay our tracks together now as luminous belonging. i am my own son.
the apple of my i becomes the unstruck note inside me, the mellow music
of a disassembled barricade resounding out, on my skin unbeaten, a little play
upon a meter shared with always more than one. it wasn't me unstrung nor out of key.
we are one on one. i feel the wonder of my birth and all its infinite potential.
i know my worth; it comes in through the ears, past go, directly to the heart.
i raise me up inside to watch the orchestra's conductor thrash around in fury.
the father tongue may still be heard but i've returned back from the pit to take
my place before the hearth and it is always warm. it's like this every day.
the voices of erasure may not ever be erased, but they don't speak for us.

apologies to all despair

i was once a sun and had the wish to sing, but it's alright
instead to write it down and never get it right. it is alright
to be unartful with the word i lost for which these words
will never be enough. it's quite alright to move through feeling
lost and let the sound of what became become a thing again.
that was the sound before division, the vision of when i came
to be - the sound that i have always made, if unbeknownst to me.
i've been unmade in every act, but now in love is my expression.
i'm on the verge with nothing left behind.

                                           there is no benefit
in this. these words do not create a thing, but neither do they mark
a passing. i speak these words for nothing, the way a bird will sing
its song - not by first diminishing the self to sing but by singing
as it steps out of the way. the dark recedes enough for light to line
the circle. in this light i take my place beside the marching band,
with gratitude for the chance to share in something greater than myself,
the chance to sound my little note and be uncaged at last.

the tongue that i once swallowed never had a name. i have been called
so many. this is the sound of my true name, and we are being sung.
together we're the heart inside the bird for whom extinction beckons.
what better time to let the world converse and with itself through us:
to let it hear itself and with no reason for the song. there's nothing
in this but the will to be itself. this is a turn to face the self, a turn
in both directions at one time. i take this turn to let a small and simple
thing be heard: the way it feels to be, like good and held, like joy and awe
and wonder at the way that time is flying. this is how it's meant to go,
the door left swinging open and the cell left still and timeless as it goes.

the mourning pages

the feeling sense is a newborn child. when it's good it's feeling
seen and heard, and by itself. this is the meaning of division.
all that mossy and enmeshed and cloudy time in other minds
was only ever dreaming. everything i dreamt about i dreamt to do
my best. i kept myself inside for them, from me and for my own
sake. what was theirs before it could be mine has always
been for them to live it through, for we are different people.
now i've been catching up on who i was, and while i'd love
for them to get it, if they don't, well, that's okay by me. i gave
it up to keep from giving up. the memory of their recrudescence
lives on in the corner of the frame. there ain't no shame in how
and slow it dragged me, or all the ways that i despaired, no shame
in all the years i never looked to see my spine curve round
in hope of just a little favour. the stars aligned for me to suffer,
and i have learned to suffer well. i leave my bones on show now,
a hollow ornithology in this trophy case for your sleepy observation:
how i got lost in all their chronological disease of labour, how i forgot
myself through their sense of being less than anybody else
remembered. i never lobbied for release. i took it all alone.
i stayed in business till it liquidated the ways that i was taught
to hate myself. the baccalaureates i paid to earn were a way
of finding out what was for them before it ever was for me. i make
the rent for lovers versed in that transaction. they need that barricade
put up against surrender. the world goes on in endless, arbitrary dying,
for all their saintly statehood, for their misbegotten wealth, their plastic
health and glaring miscommunication. there are so many first and ever
ready ones with their always ready smiles. but nothing's moving there.
and i don't wish to change the world. you cannot change the world,
but you can be inside yourself enough to blow up everything it taught you.
this is what is needed now: downhill runners and the glory of the open fire:

a glowing red inside. they kick to keep us stepping up to what they wanted us to set aside, but you can let yourself, you can let there be no other side to this but love. this is the street i'm on. the paper trail is shred and bagged and waiting for collection. i'm sitting on the kerb. i bend my head to shield the little face turned up to mine. i'm always his protection. the sun is high and warm and so i hold him now like this each day, out here on the verge.

Vancouver (so-called), 2020

This journey was undertaken as an uninvited traveller on the stolen territories of the people of the Squamish, Musqueam and Tsleil-waututh First Nations, amidst an ongoing genocide the existence of the settler-colonial state and capitalist resource extraction enterprise otherwise known as Canada is singly dependent upon, and in which my mere presence renders me complicit.

Acknowledgements

My heart beats for my grandmother, Charan, my mother, Harbhajan, and my wife, Tamara, without whom: where would I be. Thank you, dearest women, for loving me as you have.

I am filled with gratitude for my found sister, Bhanu Kapil, for showing that someone can come from where we come from but stay connected. Thank you, just for being, beloved.

I have had the good fortune to encounter two wise men, Bahram Moterassed and Sia Bandarian, who journeyed with me on my way back. Thank you both for your unique gifts.

I also want to thank Dara Khan for being kind enough to cast a caring and compassionate eye on this manuscript when in a previous form. May Nusrat always preserve you, my friend.

Finally, my unbridled appreciation for the Broken Sleep team, and especially for Aaron Kent, whose goodness shines through all that has tried to obscure it. May you continue to rise…

PROTECT YOUR UNREST

CPSIA information can be obtained
at www.ICGtesting.com
Printed in the USA
BVHW021718141222
654267BV00002B/57